THE SEC.... .
OF
KIRIBU TAPU LAGOON

Written by Tandi Jackson
Illustrated by Caroline Campbell

© 1995 Shortland Publications

09 08 07
12 11 10 9 8 7

Published in Australia and New Zealand by MIMOSA/McGraw-Hill
8 Yarra Street, Hawthorn, Victoria 3122, Australia
Published in the United Kingdom by Kingscourt/McGraw-Hill
Shoppenhangers Road, Maidenhead, Berkshire SL6 2QL

Printed in China through Bookbuilders

ISBN: 978 0 7901 1004 2

CONTENTS

KEY

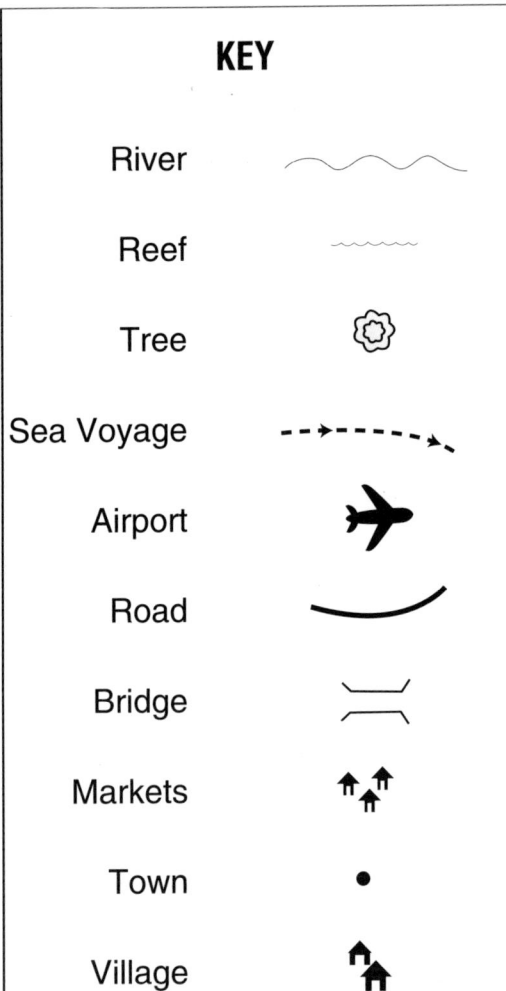

River	~~~~~~
Reef	~~~~
Tree	✿
Sea Voyage	- - -➤- - -➤
Airport	✈
Road	⌣
Bridge	)(
Markets	🏠🏠🏠
Town	●
Village	🏠🏠

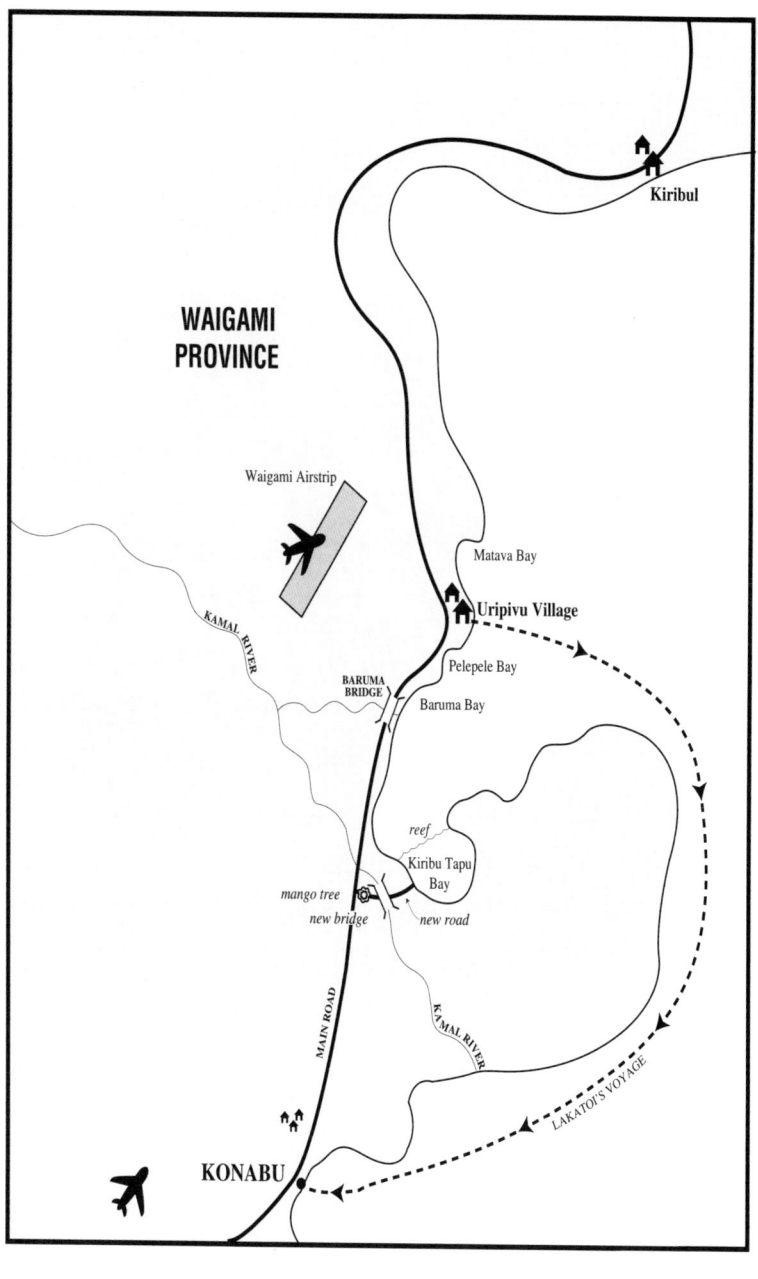

CHAPTER 1

The Arrival of Lucky

"Tell Lee to hurry up if she wants to come to the movies with us," Apu called to his friend Sare. "The PMV will be here any minute!" The PMV, a truck which was used as a bus, came bouncing along the dirt road towards the village.

Sare sprinted across the village square, leaped over the hibiscus bush in front of the Chinese trade store where Lee lived, and shouted, "Lee! Are you ready? We have to go right now!"

Sare was tall and well built and, even though he was fifteen and Lee was only twelve, they were good friends. Lee appeared at the doorway, grinning. She was half-Chinese and half-Melanesian. She had long, black hair, unlike the short, black, curly hair of her friends. She came bounding down the front steps of the trade store, wearing jeans and a pink shirt.

"Dad gave me some money for helping him in the store yesterday. I'll be able to spend it in town," she said, smiling at him.

Sare grabbed her by the hand and together they raced across the road, just as the PMV pulled up to the bus-stop. The three friends found room to sit at the back of the truck.

"Girls are always late," said Apu, who was seventeen and loved teasing Lee. "Trying to make yourself look good for those towny boys, eh!"

Lee made a face, shoved his shoulder, and turned away to look out the window at the blur of coconut trees. Sare grinned while Apu rubbed his shoulder in mock pain. The PMV continued on its bumpy ride, coming to a halt at the next village, where two people and a baby pig climbed on board.

Lee closed her eyes as the truck gathered speed again. She loved to feel the cool wind on her face. She could hear the boys talking about which movie they should see. She didn't mind what they saw – it was the art supplies store in town that fascinated her. She had decided that when she finished school, she would dedicate herself to painting full time. Lee was very creative and could always be found with a sketch-book in her hand. Perhaps one day she would even have her own studio.

Lee's father was Chinese and her mother was the village chief's niece. Mr Chang ran a trade store that provided the villagers with all the basic, everyday items they needed. Lee worked in the store after school each day for two hours, and sometimes on the weekends, which was great because she earned some spending money. But she didn't want to spend the rest of her life just standing behind a counter.

Lee's day-dreaming was interrupted by something cold and wet on her leg. Thinking it was Apu teasing her again, she kicked out with her foot. The resulting squeals made her sit bolt upright in her seat. She had just kicked the piglet. The boys and the other passengers all laughed, while the piglet's owner tried to calm the frightened creature. Lee blushed in embarrassment and mumbled apologies to the owner.

Just then Apu pointed out to sea. "Isn't that our fishing boat?" he cried.

Lee looked in the direction he was pointing, just in time to catch a fleeting glimpse of a boat before it disappeared behind the trees.

"It couldn't be," said Sare. "Mele took it up north on important business. What would it be doing down here?"

Uripivu Village, where Sare, Lee, and Apu lived, made most of its income from fishing and pearl diving. Five years before, the village people had decided to form a cooperative and buy a fishing boat that they could all use. Apu and Sare and several other young men of the village dived for pearls from the boat. Mele was the village's best fisherman and was responsible for keeping the fishing boat in running order. Apu was an expert diver and had just joined the co-op after finishing school. Sare planned to do the same when he finished school.

Living right next to the ocean meant that the sea played a big part in the children's lives. They not only learned to swim when they were babies, but they could also paddle a canoe by the time they were four years old. Very few village children drowned or got lost at sea.

"It just looked like any old boat to me," said Lee. "What makes you think it was ours?"

"Oh, Lee! I wouldn't expect you to be able to tell the difference between a boat and a bicycle," snapped Apu. "I happen to know plenty about boats. Especially *that* one because I work on it five days a week."

"You don't need to be such a know-it-all!" exclaimed Lee, twisting around towards the window.

The remainder of the trip into town was relatively quiet, each friend occupied with personal thoughts. While Lee day-dreamed about the pictures she would paint in her studio, Apu wondered what the co-op fishing boat was doing so far off course, and Sare was thinking about what movie they should see.

At last, they reached town, and the friends headed for the movie theatre. They had all agreed to see the science fiction movie that had just reached their island from the United States.

"Wasn't it scary?" said Lee, when they came out.

"Whoooo!" Apu leaped into his monster pose. "Come on, I'm starving! Let's go and get something to eat!"

They went into BP's, which stands for "Burns Philp" – the only big store in town – and each bought fresh bread rolls and a drink. As Apu paid for the food, he picked up a leaflet from a pile on the counter. "Win a TV, VCR, and video camera," he read.

"That'd be great!" said Sare, looking interested. "What do you have to do to win?"

"Fill in your name and address, answer the following questions...," Apu read out as he skimmed the form. "Not much really. Do you have a pen?"

The two boys put their heads together for a minute, filled in the questionnaire, and pushed it through the slot in the box on the counter.

"Come on, you guys! I want to go to the art store!" cried Lee impatiently.

"Right! Let's go, then!" Sare declared. "Lee's itching to spend her money."

They spent the rest of the afternoon looking in shops, playing video games, and eating ice-cream cones until it was time to catch the PMV home again. In the end, Lee decided to spend her money on some beautiful water-colour paints and a sable brush. She wanted to paint a nautilus shell that she had found on the beach last week. It was a quiet trip home, as they were all a little tired.

The next day was Saturday – no school for Lee and Sare and no work for Apu.

The friends decided to go swimming and then have a picnic at Pelepele, one of their favourite spots on the next bay down from their home. Before they left, Apu nimbly climbed a coconut palm and cut down three green coconuts, while Sare wrapped banana leaves around some cooked sweet potato left over from dinner. Lee packed cooked rice and smoked fish, and put it in her bilum with her laplap and towel, along with her sketch-book and pencil.

The friends set off down the beach, past the piles of opened oyster shells, towards the cliff path that led over the hill to Pelepele Bay. They climbed up the steep path and then scrambled down the other side. There before them was a glorious, secluded bay with sand so fine it reminded Lee of talcum powder. The sea sparkled and shimmered in the sun, looking cool and inviting.

"Come on!" challenged Sare, taking off his shirt. "Last one in's a dead fish!"

The two boys raced down the beach in their shorts and dived into the water, leaving Lee fuming on the beach. She went behind a bush to change into her laplap.

A few moments later, she heard yelling and splashing from the water. Lee charged down to the water's edge and saw the boys holding something large in the shallow water.

"I thought it was a shark!" Sare gasped. "I saw blood and thought you were yelling 'cause it had attacked you!"

"I thought it had attacked *you*!" Apu panted, gulping in relief.

"What is it?" asked Lee, looking at the dark shape in the water. "Are you guys all right?" The creature's tail flapped, spraying Lee with water.

"It's all right, Lee," Sare assured her. "You can come in. It's an injured dolphin."

Lee waded into the water next to the boys and saw that it was a dolphin – with a bloody hole in its side.

"It looks like it's been shot!" said Apu.

"Don't be silly! Who would do a thing like that? It's probably been attacked by a shark," said Lee. "It won't die, will it?" she added in a worried voice.

"Probably," Apu replied, shaking his head. "If we leave it here, a shark will almost certainly smell the blood and come and finish it off."

"I know what we could do!" said Lee brightly. "We could put the dolphin in that rock pool over there. It's always full of water, even during low tide. Then we could block off the entrance with rocks so sharks can't get in – and the dolphin won't be able to get out until it's better."

"Great idea," agreed Sare excitedly, "and we could feed it fish every day until it gets better!"

Once they'd decided on their plan, the friends worked together, carefully herding the injured dolphin towards the deep rock pool. Lee stayed and stroked its back, while the boys went off looking for big rocks to pile up at the pool's entrance. Half an hour later, the job was finished and the dolphin was safe from attack.

"I've decided to call her Lucky," Lee announced, as the boys sat down to catch their breath, "because she's very lucky to be alive." Lee stroked the dolphin's nose. "Look! She likes me!" Sure enough, the dolphin seemed to be responding to the girl's attention with a high-pitched, squealing noise.

"Lucky says she's hungry," said Lee. "Can you two catch her some fish, please?"

"What?" cried Apu. "We just had to move all those heavy rocks. *You* catch her some fish!"

"Well, I'm going to give her some of my lunch, then," said Lee, going over to her bilum. Sitting eating lunch on the rocks beside the pool, they took turns throwing pieces of smoked fish into the water. Lucky squealed with delight and caught the fish in her beak.

"So much for our lunch!" grunted Apu in disgust.

"Well, there's plenty of rice and sweet potato," Lee offered.

They spent the rest of the day playing with Lucky, and all too soon, it was time to say goodbye, and they set off back to the village, happy after a good day's work.

After church the next day, Lee, Sare, and Apu met up again to visit the dolphin.

They approached the pool cautiously, each fearing the worst. Suddenly, there was a loud squeal and Lucky's head shot up out of the water, as if to welcome them. All three jumped, almost in unison, and then broke into relieved laughter.

Over the next few days, Lee, Sare, and Apu spent every spare minute of their time with the dolphin – especially Lee, who had grown very fond of her. Once she took her sketch-book and sat beside the pool to draw her new friend.

Slowly, the dolphin's wound began to heal, and she became more friendly and playful. The friends brought her fresh fish daily, and by the following weekend, they all decided it was time to let Lucky out of the rock pool. Lee was really sad. "She'll swim off into the sea and we'll never see her again," she wailed.

"Well, it would be cruel to keep her cooped up in this small pool any longer," reasoned Apu.

Lee had to agree and, sadly, they removed the rocks blocking off the pool. Lucky darted out into the freedom of the open sea. But a couple of minutes later, she jumped out of the water and squealed at the children. Then she raced towards them, nudging Lee's legs and squealing again. The children shouted with joy.

"It looks like we won't be rid of her, after all," laughed Sare.

Apu dived into the water and swam under Lucky to tickle her belly. The dolphin called out in delight, circled Apu at the speed of lightning, and then swam underneath him, lifting him out of the water.

"Look!" cried Lee, pointing at them. "Apu is riding Lucky!"

Apu came past them, whooping and laughing as he skimmed along the water on the dolphin's back, clasping tightly to her fin. In the next instant, Lucky dived and both the boy and the dolphin vanished from sight. Lee began to panic when they didn't reappear, but Sare reminded her that Apu spent half his life under the water, diving for pearls, and could hold his breath for at least three minutes. A minute later, Lucky broke the surface of the water again, with Apu still holding on, wearing a big grin on his face.

"Hey, Lee! Sare!" he called. "Come and try this! It's great fun!"

CHAPTER 2

An Unexpected Prize

The next day after school, Lee went to Pelepele Bay to see if Lucky had come back, but there was no sign of her. She stood and looked out to sea for nearly an hour, calling her name, but the dolphin did not appear. Miserably, she finally turned away and started walking back to the village. Lucky had become so much a part of her life she would miss her.

As Lee made her way to the trade store, a van pulled up across the road, and a young man leaned out the window. "Excuse me, miss!" he called to her, looking down at a piece of paper in his hand. "Could you tell me where Apu Lepi lives, please?"

"Uh-huh," replied Lee, pointing across the village square to Apu's house. "He lives over there."

Lee wandered sadly into her house – past her father working at the counter – and lay down on her mat. She felt depressed. Would Lucky ever come back?

A few minutes later, she thought she heard someone calling her name. It was Sare. He sounded very excited. Perhaps he had found Lucky! She wiped her eyes and met him at the door of her house. He was so excited, his words tripped over each other. "The video set – a big one – a camera, and a TV, too! We won them all! Remember the competition? Isn't it amazing?"

"Sare, calm down," said Lee, shaking him. "What are you talking about?"

Apu raced up behind Sare. "He's trying to say that we won the competition at BP's," he explained. "Remember that entry form we filled in? Well, we won it. Come and have a look!"

They ran over to Apu's house. His house was one of the few village houses that had electricity. Uripivu was built beside the coast, and the houses were designed in traditional island style. Most homes were built on posts, with roofs made of sago leaf thatch and walls of sago frond midribs. Only the trade store, which was made of modern materials, and Apu's house had electricity. Lee's father ran a small generator, which provided electricity for the Chang and Lepi households.

Apu's mother was watching the man install the television and video equipment. She was shaking her head and clicking her tongue, while Apu's father sat on his mat, chewing betel-nut and spitting the bright red juice into a bowl. He was staring at the video equipment. The Lepi family had a radio in the house, but they had never seen a VCR before.

The salesman explained to the boys how the VCR worked and put on a Mickey Mouse cartoon. Before long, half the village had heard the news of the prize, and a large group had squeezed themselves into the Lepis' living-room. Small children pushed in front of the adults so they could have a better view.

"If you come outside, I'll show you how to work the camera," said the salesman. He aimed the camera at the village houses and gave the friends instructions on how to operate it. He pointed the camera at the beach and then at Sare, Lee, and Apu, moving the camera from one to the next.

They laughed self-consciously and nudged each other playfully.

"Now, let's go back inside and I'll show you what to do next," the salesman told them.

They returned to the living-room and cries of disappointment rang through the room when the cartoon was turned off – but not for long. The man showed Apu which button to press on the VCR, and suddenly, they were watching their very own village on the screen. The small children squealed with excitement, while the adults gasped. Children pointed and chanted the names of familiar objects on the screen, and when the picture swept around to the beach, everyone recognized Tane's and Sare's canoes.

Then old Tale, the oldest man in the village, appeared on the screen. He was sitting and mending the nets. Tale still used nets made from bush fibres and insisted on mending them using traditional methods, although most of the nets used by the villagers were made in Japan or Australia.

Suddenly, Lee gasped, sprang to her feet, and ran out of the room. Nobody else seemed to notice because they were now engrossed in watching the film of Apu, Sare, and Lee laughing at the camera.

They watched Apu wearing a broad smile and showing off his pearly-white teeth, Sare turning his head away shyly from the camera, and Lee covering her mouth with her hand to keep from giggling.

The film stopped abruptly and the screen went blank.

Everyone laughed, then clapped, and began chatting excitedly. After a while, they drifted reluctantly back to their houses, leaving Apu and Sare to examine their new video equipment. They were dying to try it out for themselves.

"Let's go into the village and do some filming before it gets too dark," suggested Sare.

Outside, Apu looked around for something interesting to catch on video. He filmed his mother building up the fire and his aunt opening oyster shells. He passed the camera over to Sare so he could have a turn. They walked down to the beach, and Sare turned the camera on his grandmother, who was busy making a clay pot. Her body was covered in tattoos, which was usual for women of her age. The tattoos had been a symbol of initiation into womanhood, and tattooing had been performed during the celebration of trading expeditions many years ago.

They moved the camera onto Apu's uncle, who was smoking fish on a rack over a smouldering fire.

"I'll be glad when Mele gets back with our boat," he remarked, grinning when he saw the camera pointing at him, to reveal black teeth and orange gums stained by betel-nut.

The boat! That triggered something in Apu's brain. Something to do with the fishing boat... But he lost the thought when a shout came from the water.

It was Lee. She was in the water, riding fully dressed on Lucky's back. The dolphin had come back after all.

"I saw her in the water on the video!" Lee called, as she patted the dolphin's head.

Sare joined her in the water, and the boys spent the next half-hour filming Lee and the dolphin playing together in the water.

"I'm teaching her to stop and go on command," said Lee proudly. "She's very intelligent. She seems to understand most of what I say."

Soon it was too dark to keep filming. Lee said goodbye to Lucky and went home, while the boys went inside to watch what they had just filmed.

They were very excited.

"I think I'll become a famous film producer," said Apu, thumping his chest. He had always planned to leave the village when he had saved up enough money and perhaps set up his own business.

"And I'll be your cameraman," laughed Sare.

The boys sat and watched the video. At first the film was jerky, and at one stage, they'd cut off Lee's head with the camera. As the film came to a close, Sare yawned, mumbling that it was time for bed. Apu sat up suddenly, looking very thoughtful. He went over to the VCR, pushed the reverse button, and set it on replay.

"What is it, Apu? You're not going to watch it again are you? We've got time tomorrow to play with it," said Sare.

"Shhh!" said Apu abruptly. "Just watch it carefully!"

They watched the rerun of Lucky and Lee romping in the water. The village children chased some hens and pigs along the beach. Then all they could see were the silhouettes of the coconut palms, with the sea darkening in the background.

"There it is!" Apu jumped up excitedly and pushed the pause button.

"There what is?" asked the bewildered Sare.

"The light. See it out there twinkling on the water!"

"So... Someone's out there fishing," Sare replied impatiently.

"Except that no one ever fishes there!" said Apu excitedly. "Look where the light is!"

Sare's mouth opened wide as realization dawned on him. The two boys stared at each other. "Kiribu Tapu Bay!" they both whispered together.

CHAPTER 3

A Strange Discovery

A week later, Mele returned to the village without the fishing boat. The village people gathered around to listen as he told them about how a bad storm had blown up and thrown the boat against a reef, badly holing it. He had managed to motor the damaged craft to the nearby village of Kiribul, and it was now on a slip being repaired.

"How long will the repairs take?" asked Apu's father.

"They said at least two to three weeks," Mele replied.

"But we have a large shipment of yams, smoked fish, and pearls that need to go to town this week," Uncle Rama, the village chief, said with a worried frown. It was his job to make sure that everything ran smoothly. "How will we get it there?"

"We can take it by truck," suggested Mele.

"You obviously haven't heard, Mele," said Apu. "Baruma Bridge was washed away last week by a flash flood. It will take at least ten days to be repaired."

"It was probably the same storm that hit you on the boat, Mele," said Uncle Rama.

"Oh – yes, it must have been," said Mele. "Well, there's always the lakatoi. Our village used it to trade before we bought our boat."

"But we haven't used the lakatoi for years. The sails need mending and the platform also needs some work," claimed Apu's father. "But I suppose it wouldn't be too hard to fix."

The lakatoi was a large, multi-hulled sailing canoe that had been used many years ago, mainly for trading purposes. The south-east winds blew from May to November and helped the Waigami villagers sail up the gulf to trade their pots and sago for other food and goods. This was known as the Hiri trade, and it had taken place every year during the dry season. The Waigami had traded for food while they waited for their yam harvest.

"The journey will take longer, but it should be more fun," Sare exclaimed.

"Yes, but what about the fishing trawler? How are we going to pay for the repairs, Mele? We're already a week behind with our fishing because you had the boat," remarked Nage, one of the villagers. It was obvious that he was annoyed, especially since he had been against Mele taking the boat in the first place.

"Don't worry!" Mele reassured everyone. "I have that worked out already. It was my fault that the boat was damaged, and I have already made arrangements to pay for it. I met up with some Australians who want me to fish for them further up the coast. It's night work, so I will be able to fish for the co-op during the day and put in a few hours for them each night. The money they're offering is good, and I'll soon have the repairs paid for."

"Mele, wasn't that our boat we saw down at Baruma Bay last week?" Apu asked suddenly.

"What do you mean?" Mele turned sharply and glared at Apu. "I was nowhere near Baruma Bay. I told you, I went to see friends near Kiribul."

"We went on a bus to town before the flood last week. We thought we saw our fishing boat out on the water," Sare explained. "I guess we must have been wrong."

"Of course you were," laughed Mele nervously. "One boat looks a lot like another from a distance."

The conversation changed to who would take the shipment to town in the lakatoi and when they would go.

"I'm sure he's lying," Apu murmured to his friend as they walked away from the group.

"But why? What's he hiding?" Sare was puzzled.

"I don't know," said Apu, spying his mother at work by the fire. "Come on, Sare, let's go and help smoke the tuna that we caught yesterday."

Everyone worked around the clock helping repair the lakatoi, so it was ready to launch after a couple of days. The women wove strips of palm into holes in the sails to repair them. Uncle Rama and one of his nephews bound up parts of the platform above the hull with strips of vine to give it extra strength.

The men pushed and heaved, using rollers to move the large vessel down the beach to the sea until it finally hit the water with an almighty splash. The whole village turned out for the occasion. When it was ready, the villagers loaded the cargo, consisting of smoked fish wrapped in banana leaves, yams, and pearls carefully stored in baskets woven from coconut palm leaves. The fish always sold at the markets for a good price. They tied the bundles securely to the canoe platform and carefully stowed the pearls in the hull of the canoe. As the boys were tightening the last rope, they heard a squeal behind them.

"It's Lucky!" cried Apu.

"Right on time, too!" said Sare sarcastically.

"Why do you say that?" asked Apu.

Sare waded over to the dolphin and stroked her head. "It's dinner-time, stupid!"

Apu shrugged his shoulders, not grasping Sare's meaning, and turned his attention back to knot tying. A few moments later, however, he smiled to himself as he heard Lee's voice calling the dolphin. She was coming down to the beach, carrying a basket in her hand.

"Lucky! Dinner!" Lee called.

"Dinner!" Sare mimicked her in a high-pitched voice. "Wish I were so lucky! How about some for me?"

Apu laughed and laughed as the dolphin suddenly broke away from Sare, pushing him aside so quickly that he fell over in the water. Lucky streaked through the water towards Lee, who produced a fish on cue and held it high above the animal's head.

"Dinner!" she announced again, ignoring the antics of the two boys watching her. The dolphin squealed and leaped high out of the water, catching the fish in her beak.

Apu was still laughing as Sare came up beside him, dripping wet in his clothes.

"What's so funny?" he scowled at Apu.

"You are!" chortled Apu.

As Apu followed Sare up the beach, he noticed two strange vehicles, a white Jeep and a blue truck, parked in the centre of the village. Mele was standing nearby, in deep conversation with two Australians. They spoke urgently in hushed tones, and Apu couldn't hear what they were saying.

After dinner that night, the village people gathered around a big fire on the beach. Several brought guitars, and there was singing and excited chatter about the forthcoming trip on the lakatoi. It had always been fun to go on the trip anyway, but since the village had bought the fishing trawler, the big sailing-canoe was never used.

The sight of the majestic vessel, rigged and ready for the voyage, stirred something in Apu's spirit – something he could not explain. Perhaps it was the feeling of nostalgia for the old ways, and a sadness that so many of the customs were changing.

With a good wind, it would take the lakatoi nearly a full day's sailing to reach the town, while it took only about four hours in their fishing boat. Apu remembered the last trip they had made to sell fish at the markets. It was always an exciting place to visit, a place to meet up with friends and catch up on local news.

This time, the villagers had decided that Akis and several older men of the village would sail the lakatoi, together with Akis's three sons.

As the night wore on, the singing came to an

end and the fire died down. A small group of people, including the three friends, sat staring into the fire as Uncle Rama told stories of long ago.

"Tell us about the legend of Kiribu Tapu Bay, Uncle Rama," said Sare, who loved to hear the chief's stories. He could remember sitting around the fire as a young boy, listening to the old man's stories, and even now he never got tired of hearing them.

The old man stared into the glowing embers of the fire for a long time before answering. "Many years ago, one of our ancestors entered the lagoon at Kiribu Tapu Bay in his canoe and began to fish. He decided to dive down to the ocean floor to see if there were any crayfish. Instead, he discovered treasure."

"What was it?" interrupted Lee.

"No one knows," said Uncle Rama, stirring the embers with a stick. "Legend says that he filled the canoe with the treasure, then attempted to paddle home; but he couldn't find the gap in the reef. The reef seemed to have closed in around him and risen up out of the sea like a rock wall."

"What became of him?" asked Lee, wide-eyed.

"Legend says that a huge, black monster appeared up out of the sea and devoured him. It then tipped the lagoon treasure back into the bay."

Lee shuddered and moved closer to Sare. This story always frightened her.

"Since then, no one has ever gone there. Kiribu Tapu Bay is tapu." The old man finished his story and spat into the fire.

"Have you ever seen a gap in the reef at low tide?" Apu asked him.

"I have fished in these waters all my life, as you know, Apu. I have paddled past the lagoon thousands of times, and each time I have searched for a gap in the reef. There isn't one. But at high tide, just for a short time, the reef is covered with water, and a canoe can paddle over it."

The old man reached over and picked up handfuls of sand to smother the fire.

"There is much truth in the old stories," he said quietly. "You young ones take heed!"

With those words of advice, the old man rose slowly to his feet and bade them goodnight.

Early the next morning, the lakatoi set off in a stiff breeze amid shouts and laughter from the villagers. The children squealed and splashed in the water around the canoe. Lucky was attracted by the noise and dived in front of the boat as it set sail.

The lakatoi's hull had been carved from a huge tree-trunk, and its woven sails were adorned with colourful flowers and strips of material that fluttered as the breeze caught them. The men on board tightened ropes and checked that their cargo was fastened securely. They waved from the platform built on top of the hull.

Once the lakatoi was out of sight, the three friends decided to go for a walk to a huge, old mango tree, rumoured to be a hundred years old. Lee took some empty bilums for the mangoes, while Apu carried the video camera. As they left the village, Apu noticed that the Jeep was still parked outside Mele's house.

It was a two-hour walk down the main road to the mango tree, and they all took turns carrying the camera. Every now and then, they would stop to film something interesting.

At last, they reached the big tree. It was laden with fruit. Lee began searching the ground for ripe mangoes while the boys climbed the tree. Lee found that most of the fruit on the ground was rotten, and it made a squelchy, sticky carpet under her feet.

"I'll throw you down some good ones, Lee," Sare called from above her. "Here – catch!" And he tossed two fat, ripe mangoes towards her.

Very soon, both the bilums and their stomachs were bulging with ripe mangoes. The friends wiped the yellow stains from their faces with the backs of their hands.

"I lo-o-ove mangoes!" exclaimed Lee, licking her lips.

"Here's something interesting," called Sare, as he went to pick up the video camera that was lying by a bush at the far end of the tree.

Lee and Apu went over as Sare cleared away some freshly cut palm fronds to reveal a new track. Fresh wheel marks were clearly printed in the red clay.

"Someone's gone to a lot of trouble to hide this road," observed Sare.

"Well, it's certainly very new. There's never been a road here before," said Apu, pulling at more branches concealing the road.

"I wonder where it goes," said Lee.

"Let's find out. We'll leave the mangoes here and pick them up on the way back. I'll bring the camera." Apu picked it up from where Sare had hooked it on a branch.

The three friends started along the track. After a few yards, Lee suddenly turned back and replaced the palm leaves and branches to cover the road entrance. "Just in case," she grinned, as she caught up with the others.

They followed the track for about an hour.

"Can't we go back now?" Lee complained. "My feet hurt!" She lifted her foot, which by now was covered in red clay, and rubbed it, balancing on her other foot. She wiped the clay off her hands with a leaf.

"Shhhh!" warned Apu suddenly, holding his finger to his lips. "Listen!"

They all stopped and listened carefully. The rumble of an approaching car engine echoed through the bush.

"Quick! Into the bushes!" hissed Apu.

"Why?" asked Lee. "Why do we have to hide?"

"Lee, just do it!" gasped Apu in exasperation, grabbing her by the arm and pulling her with him behind a tree.

The three were out of sight when, a few moments later, a white Jeep came roaring into view. It drove past them and disappeared around a corner. They didn't see who was driving.

"Come on! Let's follow it!" said Apu excitedly. They turned the corner and found a newly constructed log bridge across a fast-flowing, narrow river.

"This must be the Kamal River," observed Sare. "Why would anyone want to build a bridge here?"

They crossed the bridge, then noticed that it had become strangely quiet.

"The Jeep has stopped," Lee whispered.

"We've got to go carefully from now on," murmured Apu. "Something very strange is going on."

As they crept carefully around the next corner, Apu held his hand up in warning and stopped. From where they stood, there was a clear view downhill to the sea. The road ended abruptly at a small shed. There was a lot of dense jungle, but they could see the sun glinting on the water through the trees.

The Jeep was parked alongside the blue truck next to the shed. Apu recognized the two vehicles immediately. Quickly he swung the video camera onto his shoulder as three men came into view. They were too far away to be recognized, but Apu zoomed in on them with the telephoto lens and began filming.

"Can we go now?" whispered Lee in a shaky voice. "They might see us!"

They made their way back to the mango tree, collected the bilums full of mangoes, and then set off for home as dusk fell. Apu arrived home to find that his mother had gone to bed with a headache, and since the house was very small, he couldn't play the video without disturbing her. Long after Lee had left, the two boys sat outside discussing what they had seen, trying to figure out who the people were and what they were doing there. The boys agreed that it seemed pretty suspicious.

Early the next morning, Apu crept over to Mele's house. The Jeep was once again parked outside. He inspected the tires. Just as he had anticipated, the grooves were full of red clay.

CHAPTER 4

The Monster of Kiribu Tapu Bay

By asking other people in the village, Apu found out that the two Australians who had visited Mele had left the Jeep for him to drive to work and back again each night. He couldn't find out any more information about the type of work Mele was doing, other than that it was some kind of fishing.

Immediately after breakfast, Lee and Sare arrived at Apu's house to see the video. They were now able to take in far more detail of the scene they had witnessed yesterday.

"Push the pause button!" exclaimed Apu. "That looks like Mele, and the other two men are those Australians I saw him talking to in the village."

"The shed is painted dark green to blend in with the surroundings," commented Lee. "They obviously don't want to draw attention to themselves."

"It's called camouflage," said Sare.

"That's not the only thing that's camouflaged," said Apu, leaping up excitedly and pointing at the screen. "Look there – look at that shape! It looks like the outline of a boat on the water behind the shed. And that could be a jetty. It's difficult to see clearly."

Lee said what they had all been thinking. "I bet it's Kiribu Tapu Bay!"

"It must be!" agreed Apu. "When you think about the location, it couldn't really be anywhere else."

"Do you think they've found the treasure?" suggested Sare.

"Who knows," said Apu. "But it must be something really important to go to the trouble of building a new road and bridge. I wonder what they're up to."

"But Mele knows the bay's *tapu*! What's he doing there?" said Lee.

"That's what we're going to find out. I have a funny feeling about Mele Vasi!" Apu replied, looking thoughtful for a moment. "You know, it just occurred to me that this would explain why we saw our fishing boat at Baruma Bay. You have to sail past there to get to Kiribu Tapu Bay. So Mele *was* lying!"

"But what about the reef?" asked Sare. "How did they get the boat through the reef?"

"Perhaps there *is* a gap!" suggested Lee.

"Well, I'm going to visit Kiribu Tapu Bay tonight in my canoe to find out just what's going on," said Apu determinedly.

"But you can't, Apu!" gasped Sare. "It's tapu!"

"I'm still going!"

"Well, I'm coming with you, then!" said Sare bravely.

"But you won't get past the reef," said Lee in exasperation. "You heard what Uncle Rama said. There is no entrance."

"Well, I'm going anyway," insisted Apu. "If that was our fishing boat we saw on the video, they must have made it through the reef somehow!"

Late that night, the two boys, armed with torches, pushed their outrigger canoe down the beach and slid it into the water. Just as they were climbing aboard, a dark figure came scurrying down the beach towards them.

"Wait for me!" called Lee in a very loud whisper.

"What are you doing here?" whispered Sare angrily. "You're not coming with us!"

"Oh, yes I am!" Lee panted, as she waded out to the canoe and started to clamber aboard.

"But you can't!" insisted Sare. "You're too young, and it might be dangerous!"

"Sh-h-h, both of you!" said Apu. "Let her come. We might need her. But you have to keep absolutely quiet, Lee, and do what I say!"

They paddled off into the darkness. The sea was very calm, and a half moon hung in the sky, lighting their way. Halfway through their journey, Lee noticed a fin gliding alongside the canoe. She clutched Sare's arm in fear and pointed to it. Sare looked over the side and laughed.

"Since when have you been afraid of Lucky?"

At the sound of her name, a beak broke the surface of the water and moonlight lit up the friendly head of the dolphin.

"Lucky!" cried Lee in relief. "I thought you were a shark! She wants to come with us!"

"Quiet!" ordered Apu. "Remember that sound travels a long way over the water. We'll be at the reef soon, so keep an eye out for anything unusual."

They paddled for some time before sighting the reef up ahead. As they paddled closer, they looked anxiously for an opening, but the reef seemed to rise up out of the water around the lagoon like a stone wall.

"There's no opening. The legend's right," Sare whispered at last.

"But there's *got* to be," said Apu.

"We should have come at high tide – then we could have paddled over it," said Sare.

"That wouldn't have given us long enough to look around, and we might have been trapped in there," said Apu.

After more searching, the friends were about to

give up and return home when they heard a squeal from Lucky.

"Look! She's over there inside the reef!" Lee whispered excitedly. "She knows the way in."

"Quick, Lee, call her." Apu felt his heart beat faster. Lee called Lucky quietly, and the dolphin disappeared under the water, resurfacing alongside the canoe.

"Lucky can show us where the entrance is," said Apu, standing up in the canoe. "I'll climb on her back and ride her while you two paddle after us." He slid quietly into the water and climbed onto the dolphin's back. Lucky swam playfully around and around the canoe.

"The stupid animal thinks it's a game," whispered Apu angrily.

"Let me try," said Lee. "I know how to talk to her."

Lee slid into the water after the dripping Apu pulled himself back on board. She whispered something to the dolphin and climbed onto her back. To the boys' surprise, the dolphin glided off in the direction of the reef, while the boys quickly paddled after her. Before their eyes, the dolphin,

with Lee on her back, appeared to swim straight through the solid line of reef.

"It's only seaweed!" called Lee, pulling clumps of it out of her hair and clothes. "You can follow us – it's all right!"

Before they paddled through the solid mass of seaweed, Apu made a mental note of their position by lining up a large tree on the shore with a hill on the coastline. The canoe joined Lee and the dolphin inside the reef.

"Well done, Lee!" said Sare in admiration, as he helped her aboard the canoe.

"It was a good thing you came with us after all!" he continued.

"Shh! We must keep very quiet," Apu warned.

They had paddled only a short distance when Lee grabbed Apu's arm.

"Look over there!" she whispered. She pointed to the dim shape of a canoe on the water about seven metres away. The three friends froze and hoped that Lucky would be quiet while they watched and waited.

A few minutes later, something stirred in the water beside the other canoe. Their eyes opened wide in disbelief as a grotesque head rose up out of the water.

"It's the monster!" gasped Lee. "Just like the legend said!"

CHAPTER 5

A Lucky Escape

The friends stared in horror as the monster pulled itself up out of the water and onto the canoe, and hoped it hadn't seen them. They were relieved that it wasn't as big as the legend had said – in fact it seemed to be about the same size as a man.

Across the water came a voice that the children recognized.

"This blasted seaweed! It gets everywhere!"

There was no mistaking Mele's angry voice. It was only the seaweed covering Mele that had given him such a grisly appearance. The children watched him throw something into the water and then drop some heavy objects into the bottom of the canoe. After a short rest, he dived into the water, and they were able to let out sighs of relief.

"So we were right," whispered Apu. "Mele is involved in something very strange."

"I wonder what he's diving for," mused Sare.

"I bet he's found the treasure," said Lee.

The kids sat and watched for the next twenty minutes, not daring to move in case Mele caught sight of them. At last he resurfaced for the final time, climbed into his canoe, and paddled towards the shore. The children followed at a safe distance, dipping their paddles very gently into the water so as not to be heard. The dolphin's sixth sense appeared to make her cautious, and she swam very quietly next to the friends' canoe.

They reached the shore at last and pulled alongside a bank overhung with trees. Reluctantly, Lee agreed to remain in the canoe while the boys clambered onto the shore. At the same time, she felt relieved that she was staying, as she didn't like the thought of stepping onto land that was tapu. This place really gave her the creeps, but at least she had Lucky for company.

"Be careful!" she warned, her heart beating so loudly that she could hardly hear her own voice.

The boys made their way carefully along the beach and headed for the large, dark shape in front of them. On closer inspection, they found it was a fishing boat, heavily camouflaged with branches and leaves.

"They didn't want it to be seen from the water," whispered Sare. Apu shined his torch on the bow of the boat.

"It's the *Lamap* – it's our boat!" said Sare excitedly, as the beam lit up the name. "So Mele *did* lie about it being damaged."

"Mele's lied about a lot of things," agreed Apu.

A faint light was coming from the window of a small hut nearby. As they crept closer, the boys realized that the window was covered with a heavy curtain, making it impossible to see inside. The next minute, they heard voices and dived for cover as the door of the shed opened. A shaft of light fell on two men carrying heavy bags, and then the door closed behind them.

The boys watched as the men carried the bags over to the jetty and onto the *Lamap*.

"Let's go!" said Apu. "We've seen enough for now!"

As they carefully made their way back along the beach, Sare tripped over a log and let out a gasp.

"What was that?" called a voice from the *Lamap*. Two shadowy figures appeared on deck and shined torches along the beach.

Sare had hurt his ankle and was in pain. Apu, who was very strong from hauling in heavy fishing nets, quickly grabbed him under the arms and half-carried him over to the cover of some bushes. They lay very still, their hearts beating wildly, wondering what the men would do to them if they caught them. Would they find Lee, too?

The men's voices were coming closer. Strong beams of light from their torches stabbed the darkness up and down the beach. The men were almost alongside the boys when a loud squeal from the water stopped them in their tracks, only a few feet away from where the boys were hiding.

They pointed their torches towards the sea as Lucky jumped out of the water, squealed again, and swam off.

"It's only that wretched dolphin again!" said one of the men. The boys could hear the relief in his voice. "It's probably the same one I shot the other day. Thought I'd hit it, too! Come on, let's get back to work. We're all getting too jittery. No one's ever going to find us here."

"Well, we should be loaded and ready to leave for Japan by next Wednesday night," said the first man. "I won't be sorry to see the last of this place. It gives me the heebie-jeebies!"

Apu and Sare looked at each other in relief. Lucky had saved them.

"How's your ankle?" Apu whispered, when the two men were well out of earshot.

"It's sore, but I think I can make it back to the canoe," said Sare bravely.

As they were making their way back to Lee and the canoe, Apu nearly fell over a large pile of shells lying on the beach. He risked turning on the torch for a second and discovered that they were oyster shells.

"Strange!" thought Apu, picking one up and putting it in his pocket.

Lee was relieved to see the boys. She had heard the commotion on the beach and been frightened that the boys had been caught. They quickly explained in whispers what had happened, then

pushed the canoe away from the bank and quietly paddled out to sea. Further out, they realized that the tide had come in and completely covered the reef so that it was no longer visible.

"We may be able to paddle right over the top of it," said Sare.

It was a lot darker than before because clouds had drifted across the moon, making it impossible for Apu to see the landmarks that he had memorized to indicate where the gap lay.

"We'll just have to go over the top," said Apu. "Uncle Rama did say that a canoe could paddle over it at high tide." They kept paddling and cleared the reef easily.

"Thank goodness it's high tide, or we would have been in big trouble!" said Apu.

CHAPTER 6

The Letter

The next day, the friends met down at the beach to discuss their escapade. Sare's foot was much better, but he still limped slightly. As they were talking, Apu remembered the oyster shell and pulled it out of his pocket. He examined it carefully, noting that it was much larger than the ones they dived for, as well as being a different colour.

Sare produced a knife. "Open it!" he said. Carefully, Apu slid the blade into the muscle holding the sides of the shell closed, and twisted it. Sare let out a long whistle. Inside the shell lay a large pearl, which was twice the size of an average pearl and a dark gray colour.

"Black pearls!" gasped Apu excitedly. "We've

found the treasure!" The three friends knew that these were among the most valuable of all pearls.

"You mean *they* found it!" Lee corrected him.

"I wonder how many of them are down there," said Sare, lifting the pearl out of its shell. He put it in the palm of his hand and rolled it around with the tip of his finger, feeling its smoothness and admiring its round shape.

"There was a big pile of shells on the beach where I found this," said Apu. "They are usually very rare, but there must be some special conditions in this lagoon that have caused them to develop. Perhaps there are volcanic vents in the ocean floor."

"Whatever it is, they must have plenty of them by now," said Sare. "Remember we heard them say they would be ready to leave for Japan by next Wednesday evening."

"They're obviously going to try to smuggle the pearls out of the country in *our* fishing boat."

"That's not fair!" said Lee indignantly. "Kiribu Tapu Bay belongs to the Waigami people. The pearls rightfully belong to us!"

"That's right, Lee," agreed Sare.

"That rascal Mele!" seethed Apu angrily. "He must have discovered the black pearls, and then hired those Australian crooks to help him get them."

"They must be worth a fortune. We've got to stop him!" cried Lee.

Just then, there was a loud commotion further down the beach, with children shouting and people running out of their homes. The three friends looked out to sea and saw that the lakatoi was returning home.

Lee's father called her and the boys over, and asked if they would help him unload new supplies for the trade store. They watched the mighty canoe glide gracefully over the waves towards them, looking like some giant sea bird, with its large, heart-shaped sails flapping like wings as it pulled towards the shore.

Children ran into the water and surged around the boat, trying to climb up on board, while their parents reprimanded them. The village men helped pull the canoe out of the water, and everyone helped unload the boat. There were fruit and vegetables from the market, brightly coloured cloth for the women, stores of rice, bully beef, tea, and sugar. It took Lee and the boys all morning to carry the supplies up to the store.

At noon, they stopped to rest. Lee's father gave them each a can of lemonade from the store refrigerator, and Lee's mother, Tama, gave them some mumu that she had cooked the night before. It was wrapped in banana leaves, and she gave a bundle to each of the friends. Lee was her only child and she was very proud that these two young men had befriended her. She knew that her daughter was safe in their company. Lee didn't have many girlfriends, since there weren't many girls of her age in the village; and, besides that, she was something of a tomboy, quite mature for her age and preferring the company of the older boys.

Tama liked Apu very much, and thought him a very capable, hard-working young man, who was greatly respected by the village people. She considered Sare, too, a fine young man – very polite and with a great sense of humour. He had played with Lee ever since she was a small girl, and both boys were like brothers to her.

The three friends sat down on a log on the beach to eat their lunch, while Tama went back into the store. Lucky arrived on the scene, but decided she wasn't crazy about the mumu they threw her.

That night, the friends decided to search Mele's house to see if they could find anything else suspicious. Mele was something of a mystery figure. He had no living relatives in the village and no one really knew him very well. Although he was regarded as a hard worker and admired for his mechanical skills, he tended to keep very much to himself. Mele had nearly married Lee's aunt but, at the last minute, Aunt Meri had decided to marry a man from another village because Mele couldn't afford the bride-price.

After dark, they waited until Mele started up his Jeep and drove off. Apu sneaked inside the house, while Sare and Lee stood guard outside, after agreeing to whistle a warning if anyone came. Apu switched on his torch and quickly swung it around the room. The house, like many of the village houses, consisted of only one room, and the only furniture was a table, a bookshelf, and a cupboard.

Where should he start looking? He searched all the obvious places, until he found a package hidden under Mele's sleeping mat. There, wrapped in a dried leaf, was a brand-new passport with Mele's photograph and signature. Apu tore out the first page and replaced the passport under the mat; he would at least make sure that Mele never reached Japan.

Apu shined his torch along the wooden shelves one more time and picked up a lime gourd from the shelf. It rattled slightly. He tipped it upside down and another enormous black pearl fell into the palm of his hand.

Just then, Apu heard the warning whistle, and in his hurry to return the pearl, he dropped it on the floor. He was searching for it when a vehicle pulled up outside Mele's house. It was too late for him to escape out the back door, so Apu dived under the table and hid behind the tablecloth just as the front door opened.

Mele came inside and lit a kerosene lamp, filling the room with a soft glow. As Mele stood by the table, Apu spotted the pearl lying just out of his reach, in a place that Mele was sure to see it. As he was deciding whether to take a chance and grab the pearl, Mele stepped over it and went to the other side of the hut. He took out a pair of diving goggles from a cupboard. That must be what he forgot, thought Apu.

As Mele returned to the table, Apu held his breath and kept his eyes fixed firmly on the black pearl. Would Mele see it now?

Finally, Mele blew out the flame and hung the lamp on its hook, then disappeared out the door. Apu let out a huge sigh of relief. As he heard the Jeep drive off, he quickly turned on his torch and picked up the pearl, replacing it safely back inside the gourd. Then he joined his two friends waiting outside in the shadows.

"We thought you'd be caught that time!" whispered Sare.

"No, he just came back for his goggles," said Apu. "Guess what – I found another black pearl and a brand-new passport."

Sare whistled. "So he's planning on going to Japan, too!"

"Was," Apu corrected him, pulling the torn page from his pocket. "He's not going far without this!"

"That might stop *him* from getting into Japan," agreed Sare. "But they still have the pearls and the Australians can still get away with it."

"And they've got the fishing boat," added Lee. "Those rascals could just sail off with the boat and pearls without Mele. We've got to stop *all* of them!"

"I think Mele needs to be taught a lesson," said Apu. "But we have only one week to come up with a plan."

The friends spent the rest of their evening working out a strategy. The next morning they were ready to put the initial stage of their plan into action. The first thing they had to do was write a letter to the Department of Fisheries. Sare was selected for this task because he was good at writing in school. He thought very carefully and then wrote the following letter:

The Director of the Department of Fisheries
P.O. Box 7250
KONABU

Dear Sir,

I've discovered a bed of oysters bearing rare black pearls in Waigami tribal waters. My friends and I have dived for them, and we now have a large shipment of pearls that we want to sell to you. We believe these pearls are very valuable.

In return for the pearls, we would like to buy a new fishing boat from you for our village. If you could send a boat to Kiribu Tapu Bay sometime before next Wednesday night, we will give you the pearls. We can't send them by road as Baruma Bridge is still not repaired, and we are afraid to bring them to Konabu by sea in case we're robbed.

Our fishing boat, the *Lamap*, is camouflaged for this reason. It is very difficult to find the entrance to Kiribu Tapu Bay through the reef, so it would be best if you could arrive at high tide and send a dinghy across the reef to collect the pearls.

I look forward to our meeting.

Yours faithfully,

Sare read the letter to the others. "Does that sound all right?" he asked.

"It sounds brilliant!" said Apu.

"Wonderful!" smiled Lee. "Sare, you're so clever!"

Sare blushed at the compliment.

"Now it's your turn, Lee, to show us how clever *you* are," said Apu, handing her the letter. Lee raced home and got out her mother's typewriter. Tama had taught her how to type, and she often helped type out orders and accounts in the shop. She typed the letter carefully, making sure there were no mistakes.

"Excellent, Lee!" said Apu.

"Yes, well done," agreed Sare. This time it was Lee's turn to blush.

"Now the letter just needs a signature," said Apu, taking the torn-out passport page from his pocket. He stared at the photograph of Mele for a minute and said, "You're in for a big shock, Mr Mele Vasi." He studied the signature carefully and, at last, he picked up a pen and signed the name "Mele Vasi" at the bottom of the letter. The others looked at his handiwork.

Sare whistled in amazement. "No one could tell the difference!"

"Apu, you're so... " Lee and Sare started to say.

"CLEVER!" Apu finished for them. "Yes, I know. We're all so clever." They all laughed.

Sare told Lee how Apu used to get his friends into trouble at school by copying their handwriting and writing rude things about the teacher. Apu folded the letter and placed it in an addressed envelope. If they gave it to their friend Ben to be mailed today, it should get there in time. Ben's father had a business near the airstrip, and Ben often acted as the mailman for the village.

CHAPTER 7

The Great Village Clean-up

After school the following day, Apu assembled all the village children down on the beach. It was time for the second stage of their plan.

"How would you all like to see a Mickey Mouse video?" he asked them.

"Yes, sir," chanted all the children, as if they were in school.

"And how would you like to be movie stars?"

"YES, SIR!" the children shouted. They jumped around excitedly. Most of them had either seen the test run video when it first arrived, or heard about it.

"Well," continued Apu, "you can *all* see Mickey Mouse and you can *all* become movie stars, but first you all have to do something for us." The children listened as Sare told them about the importance of keeping the village clean. He explained that they needed to burn and bury rubbish to keep rats away and to stop the spread of disease. The children responded to Sare by raising their hands and telling him what they had learned at school on the subject.

Apu stepped forward again. "Now, I'm going to give out copra bags. You can work in pairs if you like – it'll probably be easier. You must half-fill the bags with oyster shells from the piles on the beach, and the other half with empty coconut shells so they don't get too heavy to lift. Then tie them at the top with string and carry them down here to the beach. The strongest among you can do all the carrying, while the others fill the bags.

"Sare and I will get rid of the bags," continued Apu. "Any other rubbish, like paper and boxes, must be burned, and cans and bottles have to be put into the rubbish pit." The children's faces were starting to fall at the thought of all the hard work.

"Now, in order for you all to become movie stars...," he continued, "I want at least thirty bags filled. Each time you fill a bag, you must tell Lee, and she'll mark it off on a piece of paper."

The children's faces brightened once again at the thought of seeing themselves on the video, and they were eager to get started. Sare divided them into pairs and gave each pair a sack, while Apu chose people to collect rubbish for burning and burying. They worked hard all afternoon, and by the end of the day, ten bags stood on the beach.

That night, Apu and Sare loaded the bags onto the platform of their outrigger. They paddled out a long way and then dumped them overboard.

The children worked hard every day after school, filling more bags. Each night, Apu and Sare would dump another load in the sea. The village people were pleased that the children were taking such an interest in keeping the village clean and tidy. By Friday, the job was finished.

The children cheered when Lee told them that they had reached their target. Apu promised that the fun would start the following day.

"Should we be putting the bags into the sea?"

Lee asked the boys that night, as they loaded the last batch of bags onto the canoe. She was very concerned about looking after the environment.

"Don't worry, Lee," said Apu. "It's all organic waste; and anyway, it won't be there for long."

That night, Apu and Sare loaded the last of the bags onto the canoe. "I hope this plan works," said Sare. "Do you think this will be enough?"

"I'm sure it will," said Apu. "It's only a narrow gap."

The next morning, all the village children crowded into Apu's house to watch Mickey Mouse. They loved it so much that they persuaded Apu to show it to them a second time. After lunch, Apu told the children to go off and play as they normally would around the village. He explained to them that he and Sare would walk around the village and film them, but that they should pretend the camera wasn't there if they wanted to look like real movie stars.

Apu, Sare, and Lee spent all afternoon filming the children. They filmed them playing football in the village square, swimming and riding on Lucky's back, playing string games, and climbing trees. The girls were very shy when they saw the camera pointing at them, while the boys showed off and acted tough.

Ben, the "mailboy", was so busy smiling at the camera that he walked straight into another boy. The two boys fell on top of each other and everyone laughed. It was so funny that Apu had to stop filming because he was laughing so hard that the camera was shaking. It was Lee's job to make sure that all the children were included in the video.

When at last they were finished, Lee asked her father for an old sign from the trade store and wrote on the back of it in large letters:

NOW SHOWING: 7:00 p.m.
The movie première of "A LUCKY ESCAPE"
EVERYONE WELCOME

Sare nailed it up outside Apu's house. They had decided to show the video in the village square since all the parents wanted to see it as well. The friends set up the video outside with a long extension cord to reach the power source in Apu's

house. Everyone helped arrange mats on the ground. There was an amazing festive atmosphere in the village that night.

Although the screen was small, it was as much of a treat as going to the drive-in movies at Konabu. Lee got her father's permission to sell popcorn, lemonade, and peanuts from the trade

store. The children dashed around excitedly while everything was being set up, until Apu told them all to go home for dinner.

At last seven o'clock arrived, and everyone in the village had assembled for the video, except Mele, who had just driven off to work. The parents were just as excited as the children and made as much noise as they did, especially when they reached the part where Ben fell over his friend.

When the video was over, Uncle Rama got up to make a speech. He thanked Apu, Sare, and Lee for the entertainment and said how much everyone had enjoyed the show. There was a round of applause. Then he thanked them for organizing the Village Clean-up Week and said that he had never seen the village look so tidy. He thanked the children for working so hard and suggested that it was something that should be done every year from now on. Everyone clapped again and then drifted off to their homes.

"Well, stage two of the plan has worked," said Sare, winking at Apu as they put away the video equipment.

Lee came running over to them excitedly. "I made $25 at my stall. Dad says I can keep $5."

"That's great, Miss Moneybags," said Apu. "Can you give us a hand putting these mats away?"

"I have to go and give Lucky her dinner now," said Lee, after they finished cleaning.

"Lee, that dolphin will get fat and lazy if you keep feeding it," said Sare.

Lee laughed. "Whoever heard of a fat dolphin! Anyway, she deserves an extra tasty treat tonight now that she's a movie star!"

CHAPTER 8

The Closed Reef

Mele was feeling extra good today. Only one more day to go in this boring village, he laughed to himself, and no one even suspected what he was up to. For a second, he felt a twinge of guilt, but he quickly pushed that feeling away. After all, he was the one who found the pearls, so he was entitled to any profits.

Mele felt under his mat to make sure that the passport was still there. He examined his packed suitcase in case he'd forgotten anything. Finally, he tipped over the lime gourd and the black pearl fell into his hand.

"Mustn't forget this one – my very first," he thought to himself as he kissed the pearl and slipped it into his pocket. Then he sat down to finish his drink.

Mele had always wanted to travel. He wondered what Japan would be like. The Australians had told him that the pearls would fetch a fortune there. Then he thought about what he would do with all the money he would have when the pearls were sold. Too bad he had to share it with the other two. Without their help, though, he would never have been able to get the pearls out of the country and, so far, their plans had gone without a hitch.

At first Mele had been troubled by the tapu, but the Australians had laughed and called it superstitious nonsense when he told them about the legend of Kiribu Tapu Bay. Perhaps he'd just travel around the world for a while before settling down in America and buying himself a big house in Hollywood next to all the movie stars.

His thoughts were interrupted by a knock at the door.

"Mele!" called Ben. "There's a letter for you!"

As Mele jumped up and opened the door, a strange uneasiness came over him. Who'd be writing him a letter? He never wrote letters to anyone.

"Thanks," said Mele, unaware of the three pairs of eyes watching him as he stood in the doorway of his house with the letter in his hand.

As he started to read, his eyes grew wider and his head started to whirl. He would have to warn the others!

Dropping the letter, he looked wildly around the house. He would have to take his things now, he thought, as he quickly reached under the mat for the passport. Stuffing it into his pocket, he grabbed his suitcase and car keys and ran out the door.

Apu, Lee, and Sare were pretending to play ball in the village square. They had been waiting for the letter to arrive because they were running out of time, since it was already Tuesday. They saw Ben heading for Mele's house and guessed he must have the letter. They watched Mele's face grow pale as he read the letter.

"This is it!" whispered Apu under his breath, as he bounced the ball to Lee.

A few minutes later, Mele ran out the door, clutching his suitcase. He jumped into the Jeep and drove off with a roar.

"I wonder what he's going to tell them," laughed Lee.

Mele had left his door open. Sare looked around to make sure that no one was looking, and then threw the ball so that it bounced through the doorway of Mele's house.

"I'll get it!" he cried in a loud voice, as he ducked inside the house to pick up the ball and the letter that was lying on the floor. He raced out grinning, and ran over to a nearby tree to read the letter to the friends.

"It worked! It worked!" shouted Sare excitedly. "They're sending a boat this afternoon at five o'clock."

"Time to put stage three into action," said Apu.

The older boy had already asked his father if he could borrow the Jeep to collect firewood, so they had axes and saws in the back of the truck in preparation. Apu called to his father that they were going, and Lee went to ask her mother if she could accompany the boys. Fishing the keys from his pocket, Apu jumped into the driver's seat. Lee came running back from the trade store and she and Sare scrambled into the front seat next to him.

They headed for the old mango tree. The track off the main road was very rough, and Apu had to put the vehicle into four-wheel drive. When they reached the mango tree, the entrance to the new road was no longer hidden by palm leaves. Mele had obviously been in too much of a hurry to bother with hiding his tracks this time. The track was muddy and slippery from the night's rain and the vehicle slid all over the place, but they managed to reach the bridge without an accident.

There was no one in sight, so Apu and Sare got out and started to pull at the logs on the bridge. Lee acted as the lookout. The logs were heavy and hard to move, but between them, they managed to move four of them and create a huge gap in the middle of the bridge, making it impossible for vehicles to cross.

"Now that we have the firewood, we may as well chop it up," laughed Sare, as he unloaded the tools. Lee got out of the Jeep and went to help. It was hard work and the logs were thick, but after several hours, they managed to cut them into pieces small enough to load onto the back of the vehicle. The three wiped the sweat from their faces. Lee chopped the top off a green coconut and they all took a refreshing, long drink. By the time they had loaded the tools onto the back of the Jeep, it was 3:00 p.m. They drove home in silence, each wondering what the next few hours would hold for them.

Apu's father was delighted to see the logs, and surprised that they had worked so hard. They stacked the logs against the side of the house to kill more time, but they still had an hour to fill before the boat arrived.

At 4:45, they saw a Fisheries boat out at sea, heading for Kiribu Tapu Bay. The friends launched their canoe, wanting to be there to make sure their plan worked. As they paddled towards the reef, the gap between them closed and the friends could see two men in uniform on the deck.

As they neared the reef, the children couldn't help but laugh. There was the *Lamap*, still covered in twigs and branches, motoring up and down inside the reef, trying desperately to find a way out. It was right on high tide and the reef was barely covered by water.

"I don't understand it!" sobbed the terrified Mele. "It's just as the legend said. I should never have come here in the first place!"

"Stop babbling, you fool!" said Bob, one of the Australians. "Of course there's a way out. We came through it when we brought this tub into the bay."

"No! It's closed up to trap us, just as it did to my ancestor before he was eaten by the monster!" wailed Mele in terror.

"Don't be an idiot, Mele! There is no monster. That's just a silly superstition," said George, the other Australian. "A reef can't just close up!"

"Oh no!" cried Bob, pointing out to sea. "Look out there! We're too late!"

They watched helplessly as the large Fisheries launch drew alongside the reef and dropped anchor. One of the men on deck was holding a loud hailer.

"Ahoy there, *Lamap*! Stand by, we're sending a dinghy over for the pearls!"

The two Australians looked at each other in disbelief, then turned on Mele.

"You set us up!" they spat at him.

"No, I didn't! Honestly!" protested Mele. "I don't know how they found out, but I had a letter from them this morning. That's why I suggested we get away earlier. I didn't tell anyone. I don't know how they found out!"

A few minutes later, the dinghy drew alongside and the Fisheries inspector climbed aboard.

"Are you Mele Vasi?" asked the inspector.

"Yes," replied Mele in a quavering voice, expecting to hear that he was under arrest.

"I'm very pleased to meet you," said the inspector pleasantly, shaking his hand. He turned to the two Australians and held out his hand.

"Don't I know you two guys from somewhere?" he said. "You look familiar."

The two Australians shook hands, but looked very uncomfortable and hastily assured the inspector that they had never met him.

"I can't wait to see the pearls. Where are they?" asked the inspector. Mele had no choice but to show him the pearls in the hold. The inspector couldn't believe his eyes when he saw the sugar sacks full of them.

"What treasure! They're magnificent," he said breathlessly, running his hands through them. "They'll be worth a small fortune."

Mele was speechless. The man appeared to be friendly towards him; but Mele had no idea what was going on, so he decided to keep his mouth shut and say nothing. The two Australians decided to do the same.

"We'll load this lot on board the dinghy now. Three or four trips should do it. Would you fellas give me a hand? We don't want to drop them in the sea now, do we!"

The dinghy was loaded and driven back to the launch, while the friendly inspector stayed and chatted with Mele and the two Australians, asking questions about how they found the black pearls. George and Bob tried their best to sound normal, but Mele was struck dumb.

"Strangely enough," said the inspector, "I can remember once hearing some crazy legend about this place. I don't remember any details, though."

Apu, Sare, and Lee kept their distance and pretended to be fishing from their canoe. They watched the Fisheries launch drop anchor and the two men motor across to the *Lamap*. Lucky had joined them and was swimming around the canoe, hoping for a tidbit or a game.

"Go away, Lucky," Lee scolded. "This isn't the time for a game!" As always, the dolphin obeyed Lee and swam off.

They watched as the first load of pearls was taken across the reef towards the launch and noticed that one of the men stayed on board the *Lamap*.

"Good!" said Apu. "That means they won't be able to hide any of the pearls."

The children waited until they were certain that all the pearls had been transferred to the launch, then slowly paddled away, checking that the launch pulled up anchor and motored off. They also heard the engine start on the *Lamap* and watched it motor back into shore.

"I wouldn't like to be in Mele's shoes now," said Sare, as they paddled for home.

"The best is yet to come," laughed Apu. "Imagine their faces when they try to escape over the bridge." They all laughed.

"I do feel a bit sorry for Mele," said Lee after a while. "He's done some good things for our village over the years."

"Well, if he hadn't been so greedy, he wouldn't have been in this mess!" said Apu in a harsh tone.

CHAPTER 9

The Rescue

Mele did not return that night. When there was still no sign of him the next morning, the friends began to worry.

"Those crooks might have murdered him!" said Lee with concern.

"Yes, I've been thinking the same thing," said Sare.

"We'll wait one more night," decided Apu. "If he isn't back tomorrow morning, we'll go and look for him at high tide."

Mele did not return. Early the next morning, before anyone else was awake, the friends prepared to visit Kiribu Tapu Bay. Fortunately, high tide was at first light, so no one from the village saw them heading for Kiribu Tapu Bay.

The friends reached the reef just as dawn was breaking, and paddled easily over the reef at high tide. The *Lamap* was tied up at the jetty, but the two vehicles had gone and the place was deathly quiet.

"I'm scared," whispered Lee. "What if the Australians are still here?"

"I doubt it. The vehicles aren't there, which means they've probably gone, too," said Sare. "Mele might have gone with them, of course."

"I doubt that!" said Apu. "Where would he go?"

"They would have had to abandon the vehicles at the broken bridge," said Lee. "What will happen to them?"

"I'm sure they'll be very useful, Lee," smiled Apu, winking at Sare. "We'll go and repair the bridge, and drive them back to the village once we get the *Lamap* home."

"But how will you explain it to everyone in the village?" Lee insisted.

"We'll think of something," said Apu.

The friends pulled their canoe onto the beach and went to search for Mele. They pushed open the door of the hut, but the place was empty, except for some copra bags and a few shells.

"Let's try the boat," suggested Sare. They walked along the jetty and onto the deck of the fishing boat. As Apu pushed open the cabin door, they heard a moan and found Mele lying on the cabin floor, bruised and beaten. He looked awful.

"Mele, it's all right! It's only us," said Apu gently, kneeling beside the injured man.

"Oooh!" moaned Mele.

"Someone get some water," ordered Apu.

Sare found a bowl and filled it with water. Mele drank from it thirstily. Lee tore up an old rag and knelt down beside Mele. She washed away the blood on his head and found a large gash. Fortunately, it wasn't too deep and had stopped bleeding. He was also covered in bruises.

Lee had taken a first aid course and, after checking for broken bones, she decided he wasn't hurt too badly.

"You're very lucky, Mele," she said. "We thought they'd killed you."

Mele stared at her. "You... you mean you know what happened?"

"We know almost everything, Mele," said Apu.

"So it was you who...," Mele winced in pain as he tried to sit up.

"Take it easy," said Sare, helping him to sit up. "We found out what you were up to and decided to put a stop to it."

"Oh," groaned Mele again. Lee held the bowl to his lips and he took another drink.

"You know, you're very lucky to be alive," said Sare.

"You're also very lucky not to be in prison," added Apu.

Sare made them all a cup of tea and Lee found something for him to eat. He was soon sitting up by himself and feeling much better, except for his aching head.

"What day is it?" he asked.

"Thursday," said Lee.

"Then I've been lying here for..." said Mele, trying hard to think.

"Must be nearly two days," said Apu. "I suppose your friends beat you up and then took off in the vehicles."

"How did you find out?" asked Mele. Apu told him how they had discovered what was going on at Kiribu Tapu Bay.

"We want to know how you found the treasure, Mele," said Lee.

"I was fishing by the reef one day when a large school of tuna leapt out of the water in front of me. It was low tide and the reef was sticking out of the water. A short while later, I saw the tuna jumping around inside the reef, so I decided to follow their trail and that's how I found the gap in the reef. It was covered with heavy seaweed," said Mele.

"Yes, we know. We found it, too," said Apu.

"But now it's gone!" cried Mele, as he remembered what had happened. "We tried to escape but the gap had closed up, just as the legend said it would. Perhaps it was because we broke the tapu. We couldn't get out of the bay."

Apu was tempted to let Mele believe that was the truth, but he thought he'd probably been punished enough.

"That was because we blocked up the gap to stop you from leaving," said Apu. "Remember the

Village Clean-up Week we organized? Well, we dumped all those bags of shells in the gap to close up the reef."

Mele actually looked relieved. "I was sure we'd angered the gods by breaking the tapu. But what are you going to do with me now?" he asked dejectedly. "Hand me over to the police, I suppose."

"Well, I suppose we should," said Apu. "But you're the only one in the village who knows about engines. If we lost you, we'd have no one to fix our vehicles and fishing boats. If you do exactly as we say, Mele, no one else will ever discover what really happened."

"You do deserve to go to prison, though, Mele Vasi," said Lee angrily. "Those pearls belonged to all of us!"

CHAPTER 10

The Storm

"The first thing we have to do is get the fishing boat back to the village."

"How are we going to sail it through the reef?" asked Mele.

"All we have to do is remove the copra bags that we used to block the gap in the reef. Let's clean up this boat before we sail it, though," said Apu.

Mele obediently helped the friends clean off all the leaves and branches that had been used to camouflage the boat. Sare found a broom and swept the deck.

"How are you feeling now, Mele?" asked Apu when they had finished.

"I've still got a bit of a headache, but otherwise I'm fine."

"Good," said Apu. "Then you can start up the boat. It looks like a storm's heading this way." Everyone glanced up at the sky, where black clouds were gathering overhead. They fastened the canoe to the back of the fishing boat behind the dinghy, and Mele started the engine. The boat slowly chugged out from the jetty, heading for the reef.

"How are we going to move the copra bags?" said Lee.

Apu suggested using the winch, normally used for pulling up fishing nets. As they approached the reef, Mele threw out the anchor.

"OK, Mele and I will get in the water. We'll hook the rope to the bags, and Sare can operate the winch and lift them up out of the water onto the deck," said Apu.

"What about me?" cried Lee. "I want to help!"

"You can watch!" said Apu, as he and Mele dived into the water.

Lee, who didn't like being left out of things, jumped into the water as well. The sea was getting rougher as Mele and Apu stood on the reef and hooked the end of the winch rope to the copra bags. Sare operated the winch and the bags were lifted slowly onto the boat.

There were only a few bags to go when Mele felt a nudge against his leg and turned around to see the body of a large "fish" swimming away from him. He dropped the sack he was guiding and reached for his knife. Apu saw the look of terror in Mele's face as the fish turned and started swimming back towards them through the now murky, rough water.

Mele swam to the surface, screaming, "There's a shark down there! Lee, get in the boat quickly while I kill it!" He pulled out his knife.

Lee screamed out, "No! Mele, it's not a shark. It's our pet dolphin – she won't hurt you."

Mele hadn't heard. Realizing what was happening, Sare jumped into the water to help, and Apu and Lee swam after Mele to stop him. Mele was just about to stab Lucky in the side, when the dolphin swerved at the sound of Lee's voice shouting above and surfaced near her. Apu swam over to Mele and grappled with the knife in his hand, shaking his head at the same time.

"It's only a dolphin!" screamed Lee. "She's our friend, Mele. You could have killed her!" Lucky poked her head out of the water and squealed. She nodded her head as if she were agreeing with Lee.

"I thought it was a shark!" spluttered Mele. "I couldn't see under there."

"We'd better hurry," said Apu. "The sea's getting choppier. There are only a couple more bags to move and then we should be able to get through the reef. One more dive should do it. Lee, you get on board now; it's getting too rough."

There was a loud clap of thunder, and rain started to pour down. Apu dived down to secure the winch hook to the last bags, and Lucky helped by pushing at the bags with her nose. When they finished, everyone scrambled back on board the *Lamap* and dried themselves, while Mele started the engine. Sare pulled up the anchor and called to Lucky to keep away from the propeller.

"What are we going to do with the bags now?" asked Sare.

"We'll drop them off at Matava Bay and use them as a fence around the gardens to keep out the wild pigs," said Apu. "No one at Uripivu will be able

to see us because of the storm. If the weather clears, it'll look as though we've come from the north."

The fishing boat chugged its way slowly through the gap in the reef, parting the thick seaweed, as the rain pelted the cabin window, making it hard to see.

"What am I going to say to everyone when we get back?" asked Mele.

"Well," said Apu, who had it all worked out, "you can say we were out fishing when we saw you approaching and got a lift home with you. You have been away for several days because you had a letter from your friends at Kiribul, the letter Ben gave you, saying that the boat was repaired, so you went to fetch it back. You didn't tell anyone because you wanted it to be a surprise."

Mele marvelled at the cleverness of these young people. They had certainly outsmarted him. Another huge clap of thunder exploded in the sky above them. The waves were growing larger, and the fishing boat bounced up and down like a cork on the ocean. They were heading north past Uripivu Village to Matava Bay. It was so black that they could hardly see land.

"Can you see where we're going, Mele?" asked Lee.

"Don't worry, I've sailed in weather far worse than this, and I know these waters like the back of my hand."

"Just as well the hull wasn't really damaged," said Lee.

"What if someone asks to see the repairs to the boat?" said Mele.

"You're the only one who ever looks at the engine. No one else has any reason to pull up the floorboards – they'll believe whatever you tell them," claimed Apu.

"You've thought of everything, haven't you?" said Mele.

"We're a pretty good team," Apu agreed, smiling at the others.

The storm suddenly disappeared as quickly as it had come, and the sun emerged just as Matava Bay came into view. It was the rainy season, and it often poured like this each day for an hour and then stopped as suddenly as it started.

They landed and began to unload the copra bags. This time, Mele and Lee stayed on board and winched the bags down to Sare and Apu, who carried them up onto the beach. It was hard work and took some time to unload.

"We'll come back another day and use them to fence off the gardens," said Apu. "I'm too tired to do it now!" They set off again in the *Lamap*, heading for Uripivu Village. It was noon, and they could see people gathering on the beach as they motored slowly into the bay.

Apu had told his father that they needed to borrow his Jeep to take Mele to Kiribul to collect the vehicle he'd left there. It would take them nearly all day to rebuild the bridge and collect the two vehicles. Mele and Sare could drive them back and Apu would drive the Jeep. It would take the same amount of time to drive to Kiribul and back, so it was a good alibi.

They loaded saws and axes into the Jeep and set off. When they reached the bridge, they saw the two abandoned vehicles waiting on the other side.

"I hope they left the keys in them," said Sare.

"I brought a spare set in case they didn't," Mele responded.

They chose some suitable trees nearby and started the laborious job of cutting them down.

"I wonder what happened to the two Aussies," said Apu, as he took a rest from chopping through a thick trunk.

"They probably ran like scared cuscus!" said Sare.

"I doubt that we'll ever see them again," said Mele. "They think I reported them to the police. No doubt they're on their way back to Sydney by now."

"There'll be no problem with our keeping the vehicles, then," said Apu.

"How will we explain them to everyone?" asked Lee.

"I could say that my Australian friends had to return to Sydney urgently, and asked me to look after the vehicles for them," suggested Mele.

"Sounds good to me," said Sare. "Too bad if they never come back to get them!"

"Yes, too bad," agreed Apu, "as long as everyone in the village with a driver's licence is able to use them, Mele."

"That's OK by me," agreed Mele.

They kept on chopping. Lee had gathered some mangoes from the nearby tree and they stopped to eat. The felled logs were rolled onto the bridge and fastened to the main supporting logs with strong vines, and at last, the bridge was finished.

They walked over the bridge and found keys in both of the vehicles. Sare drove the blue truck carefully over the bridge, but they had done a good job and there were no problems. The group set off for home in a convoy of vehicles, back along the muddy track that led to the mango tree. The village had suddenly increased its vehicles from one to three.

"Not bad for a day's work," thought Apu to himself.

CHAPTER 11

A Gift from the Gods

A week later, Apu's father came home after a day's fishing in a state of great excitement.

"There's a gap in the reef at Kiribu Tapu Bay!" he exclaimed.

Everyone gathered around to listen to his story. People clicked their tongues and shook their heads in amazement. Uncle Rama was considered to be the wisest man in the village. When he heard the story, he nodded his head in understanding and interpreted what it meant.

"The tapu on Kiribu Tapu Bay has been lifted at last. Last week I heard a loud noise like thunder, but the sun was still shining. It came from the direction of Kiribu Tapu Bay. It must have been the gods taking their treasure from the bay and opening up the reef. From now on, we can go to the bay, and it will be called just Kiribu Bay."

Apu, Sare, and Lee looked at each other knowingly.

"There was one other thing I remember about the legend," added Uncle Rama, scratching his head, "but it still doesn't make sense."

"What is it? Tell us!" said everyone eagerly.

"Well, the story also said that when the tapu was lifted, the gods would send the Waigami people a gift to thank us for honouring the tapu for so many years and guarding the treasure."

Many of the people listening gasped, but some of the younger ones tried to cover their smiles. They didn't believe most of Uncle Rama's tales. However, they did respect the old man, since he had always shown himself to be a wise and brave chief of the Waigami people.

That afternoon, a brand-new fishing trawler arrived by sea at Uripivu Village, accompanied by a smaller boat. A man came ashore with some papers and asked for Mele Vasi. Everyone gathered around Mele and the stranger.

"I have been told to deliver this new boat to Uripivu Village," he said.

"But where did it come from?" asked Mele in surprise.

"I know nothing about it," said the man. "I was only told to deliver the boat to Uripivu Village and to give the ownership papers to you. You'll find the boat fully equipped with all the latest fishing gear. These papers will also tell you everything you need to know about how to operate the boat."

He was about to walk back to his dinghy when he turned to Mele again and fished inside his jacket pocket. "I almost forgot. The Fisheries inspector asked me to give you this letter, too." He rowed back out to the smaller launch and they motored off, leaving the brand-new trawler anchored in the bay. The villagers stared at the gleaming vessel in disbelief. It was twice as big as the *Lamap*. No one spoke for a long time.

Just then, Lee spotted Lucky. She jumped right out of the water next to the new trawler, squealed, and did a somersault. She was followed by two more dolphins, and then another three appeared. Suddenly, the sea seemed to be full of dolphins, and the villagers watched in awe, since dolphins had always been considered a sign of good luck.

Uncle Rama broke the silence.

"I am an old man and soon I will die. I am privileged – indeed we are all privileged – to be here to receive the gift that the gods promised our people many moons ago. The gods know that our survival depends on the sea, and this new boat will be a great asset to us.

"Today I have also had a prayer answered. Something has been resting heavily on my heart for some time and I have not known what to do. As you all know, I do not have a son, and I have not known who to choose as my successor. But the gods have chosen for me. Your new chief will be Mele Vasi," said the old chief.

"Mele has proved himself worthy," he continued. "He's spent the last two weeks doing extra work to pay for repairs to our old boat. He's always been one of our best fishermen, and he has much knowledge about fixing engines. The gods sent the boat papers to him and they have chosen well."

The village people cheered and patted Mele on the back. Mele glanced sheepishly at the three

friends standing nearby. He couldn't believe what he was hearing, and neither could they. Instead of being punished, Mele was being treated like a hero. Should they expose him for the rascal he really was?

On the other hand, perhaps he had learned his lesson. Many thoughts flashed through Apu's mind. Mele had been given a nasty beating and his skills *did* benefit the village people. In earlier times, the chief decided on the punishment of a criminal. Sometimes, depending on the crime, a criminal was forgiven and given a second chance. Perhaps they should give Mele another chance.

When all the excitement had died down, Mele joined the three friends on the beach.

"I know what you're thinking," he said to them solemnly. "I don't deserve any of this. I guess it was you three who traded the pearls for the new boat. I want you to know that I am truly sorry for what I've done, and I promise to be a good chief to the Waigami people. If you expose me, who will look after the two fishing boats? And who will fix the vehicles? I implore you to at least give me a chance to prove myself."

The friends looked at Mele, not knowing what

to say. At last Apu spoke.

"All right, Mele, you can have your chance," he said quietly. "But just in case you ever decide to be treacherous again, I had better warn you that the truth will come out. We have proof of what happened on video tape."

"Don't worry, Apu," said Mele. "Now I have every reason to do my best for my village and my people, and that's what I intend to do." He suddenly remembered the letter he had been given and opened it.

"It seems my Aussie friends didn't get off so lightly, after all," he said, frowning.

"The Fisheries man that was here the other day thought he recognized them and made some inquiries at the police station. It seems they've tried something like this before and were wanted by the police. They were arrested in Konabu as they were about to board a plane to Sydney. He says I was lucky they hadn't tried to rip me off and wishes me luck with the new fishing trawler."

"Good!" said Apu. "They deserved to be put away."

"Lucky it wasn't you, Mele!" said Sare seriously.

A week later, there was great feasting and rejoicing. In the old days, there was always a ceremonial platform, called a dubu, in the centre of the village. When somebody harvested a large number of yams or raised many pigs, they would arrange a feast, accompanied by dancing and singing, on the dubu. These days, however, the village church was called a dubu, because in many ways the church had taken a central place in the communal life of the village.

However, there were still occasions when feasts and celebrations were held, and Uripivu Village had much to celebrate between the gift from the gods and the appointment of a new chief.

When night fell, everybody gathered around to watch the outgoing chief, Uncle Rama, present Mele with the woven cloak and carved club that had been given to him by his father. As the men of the village started beating their drums, young men came out of the dark shadows wearing their traditional dress of aprons made from tapa cloth with traditional designs painted on them. Their bodies and faces, covered in pig grease and ochre, gleamed in the firelight as they danced around blazing fires. They wore highly prized kina shells around their necks, and head-dresses made from bird of paradise feathers. The young men swayed and stamped their feet, chanting in time to the rhythm of the drums.

Apu and Sare were among the dancers. It wasn't often these days that they danced wearing their traditional dress, but they found it very exciting and almost magical. It was part of their culture and they were proud of it. The Waigami were a people living in the modern world, but it was good to celebrate their roots and the customs of their ancestors.

The women, who had been preparing the feast for days, set out an array of wonderful-smelling food on rows and rows of banana leaves. There were mumus, containing grated yam, pig meat or fish, and coconut milk, which had been cooked under hot stones in pits under the ground; as well as baskets of vegetables, such as cooking bananas, breadfruit, taro, and yams. Other baskets contained large coconut crabs, crayfish, oysters, and fish. It was a feast to remember, and everyone ate until they could hardly stand.

Lee joined the other young girls in a dance. Although she was half-Chinese and had straight, black hair, everyone in the village accepted her as a Melanesian and she enjoyed the best of both cultures. Lee wore the grass skirt her mother had made her and flowers in her hair. Her face was painted, and layers of brightly coloured beads hung around her neck. She smiled at Apu and Sare as she danced past them. It was all so exciting. As she danced past Mele, he gave her a nod. Lee understood that it meant thank you.

GLOSSARY

betel-nut – a nut chewed by islanders that stains the teeth

bilum – a colourful string bag

bride-price – the money or goods a man's family must pay to the woman's family before he can marry her. Today, it is paid in money and food, but many years ago, it was paid in pigs, kina shells, and yams.

bully beef – tinned beef

cooperative or co-op – a business shared by a group of people. The profits are shared equally.

copra bag – a string bag that is used to hold copra (smoked coconut kernel)

coral reef – a ridge or bank in the sea near land, made up of sand and coral

cuscus – a possum

dubu – a ceremonial platform used for feasts

Hiri – a trading expedition

kina shell – a large shell used as currency

lagoon – a piece of water separated from the sea by a coral reef

lakatoi (pronounced lak-a-toy) – a large sailing canoe used for trading purposes

laplap – a colourful piece of material that islanders use to wrap around their bodies

Melanesia – the islands of the West Pacific

mumu (pronounced moo-moo) – traditional food, such as yam and pig meat, cooked by hot stones under the ground

outrigger – a long piece of wood, attached by sticks to one side of a canoe, that sits in the water and helps balance the canoe

PMV – the abbreviation for a Passenger Motor Vehicle, or a truck used as a bus

rascal – a modern pidgin English word used to describe a criminal

tapa cloth (pronounced tar-pa) – a cloth made from the bark of a tree, which is beaten with a club. It is painted when it dries.

tapu (pronounced tar-poo) – a place or a thing forbidden to people

trade store – the name for a trading post throughout Melanesia

village – a small group of houses where people from the same ancestry live. There may also be a school and a church located there.

TITLES IN THE SERIES

SET 9A

Television Drama
Time for Sale
The Shady Deal
The Loch Ness Monster Mystery
Secrets of the Desert

SET 9B

To JJ From CC
Pandora's Box
The Birthday Disaster
The Song of the Mantis
Helping the Hoiho

SET 9C

Glumly
Rupert and the Griffin
The Tree, the Trunk, and the Tuba
Errol the Peril
Cassidy's Magic

SET 9D

Barney
Get a Grip, Pip!
Casey's Case
Dear Future
Strange Meetings

SET 10A

A Battle of Words
The Rainbow Solution
Fortune's Friend
Eureka
It's a Frog's Life

SET 10B

The Cat Burglar of Pethaven Drive
The Matchbox
In Search of the Great Bears
Many Happy Returns
Spider Relatives

SET 10C

Horrible Hank
Brian's Brilliant Career
Fernitickles
It's All in Your Mind,
    James Robert
Wing High, Gooftah

SET 10D

The Week of the Jellyhoppers
Timothy Whuffenpuffen-
    Whippersnapper
Timedetectors
Ryan's Dog Ringo
The Secret of Kiribu Tapu Lagoon